PIANO • VOCAL • GUITAR

GRATEFUL DEAD
THE DEFINITIVE COLLECTION

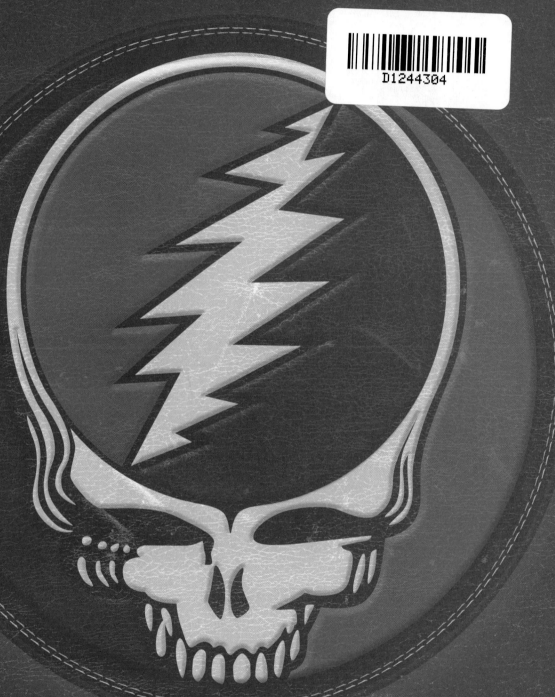

ISBN 978-1-4950-0695-1

HAL•LEONARD®
CORPORATION
7777 W. BLUEMOUND RD. P.O. BOX 13819 MILWAUKEE, WI 53213

Visit Hal Leonard Online at
www.halleonard.com

CONTENTS

ALABAMA GETAWAY

Words by ROBERT HUNTER
Music by JERRY GARCIA

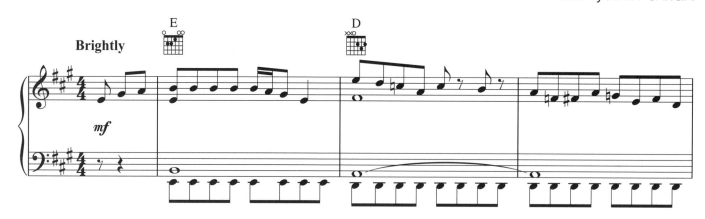

Thir-ty-two teeth_ in a jaw-bone;
Ma-jor Do-mo Bil-ly Bo-jan-gles   sat
Ma-jor said, "Why_ don't we give_ him

Al-a-bam-a try-in' for none._   Be-fore I have to hit him,   I
down and had a   drink_ with me._   Say, what a-bout Al-a-bam-a?   It
rope e-nough to hang_ him-self?_   No need to wor-ry the ju-ry; they'll

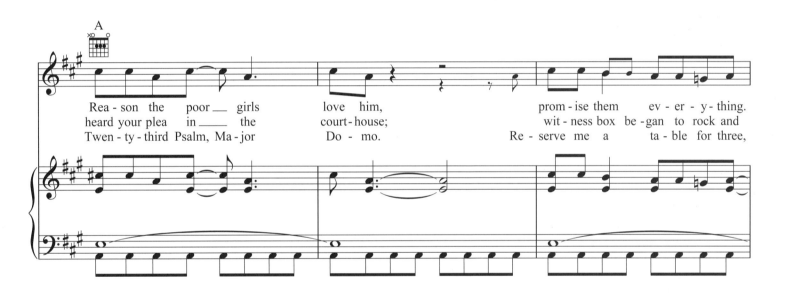

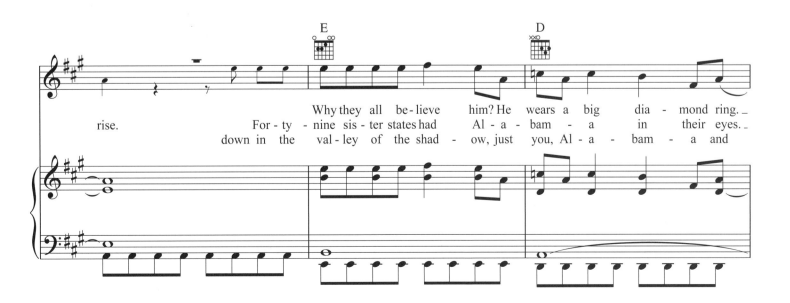

ALTHEA

Words by ROBERT HUNTER
Music by JERRY GARCIA

Set - tle back; ___ eas - y, Jim." ___

Additional Lyrics

2. You may be Saturday's child all grown,
   Moving with a pinch of grace.
   You may be a clown in the burying ground
   Or just another pretty face.
   You may be the fate of Ophelia,
   Sleeping and perchance to dream,
   Honest to the point of recklessness,
   Self-centered to the extreme.

3. Ain't nobody messin' with you but you.
   Your friends are getting most concerned.
   Loose with the truth, maybe it's your fire,
   But, baby, don't get burned.
   When the smoke has cleared, she said,
   That's what she said to me:
   You're gonna want a bed to lay your head
   And a little sympathy.

4. I told Althea I'm a roving sign,
   That I was born to be a bachelor.
   Althea told me, "Ok, that's fine."
   So now I'm out trying to catch her.
   I can't talk to you without talking to me.
   We're guilty of the same old thing.
   Thinking a lot about less and less
   And forgetting the love we bring.

ATTICS OF MY LIFE

Words by ROBERT HUNTER
Music by JERRY GARCIA

In the ___

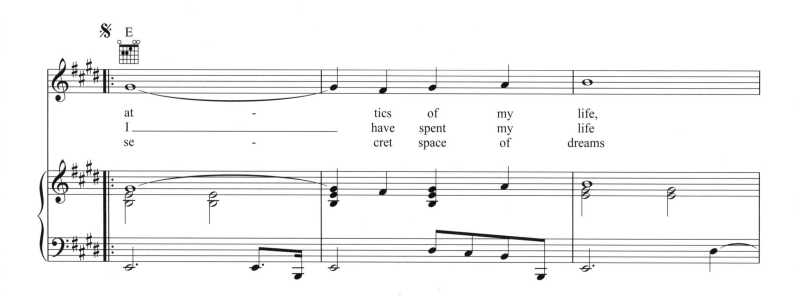

at - tics of my life,
I ___ have spent my life
se - cret space of dreams

BERTHA

Words by ROBERT HUNTER
Music by JERRY GARCIA

Brightly, in 2

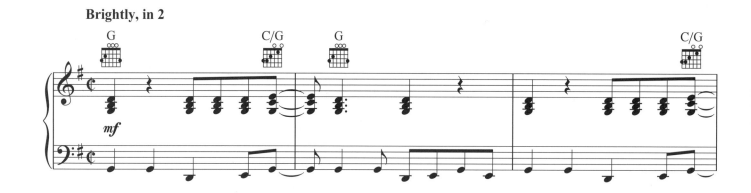

I ___ had a hard ___ run, _____
\- storm, _____

run - nin' _____ from your win - dow.
Lord, I went down in - to the sea. ___
ducked in - to a bar ___ door.

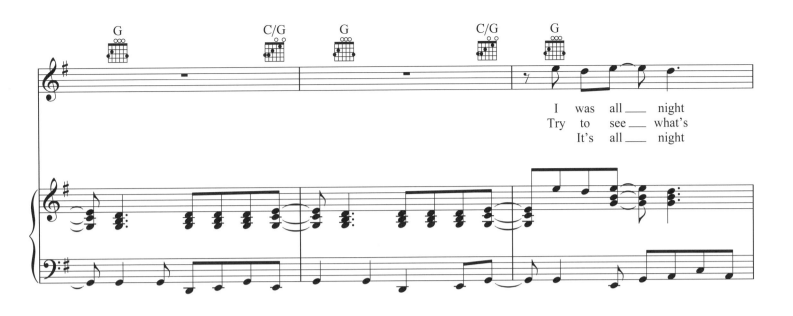

I was all ___ night
Try to see ___ what's
It's all ___ night

run - nin', _____ run - nin'. Lord, _____ I
go - in' _____ down, _____ try _____ to
pour - in', _____ pour - in' rain, Lord, _____ but

won - der if you care. _____
read be - tween the lines. _____
not a drop on me. _____

BROKEDOWN PALACE

Words by ROBERT HUNTER
Music by JERRY GARCIA

sing - ing _____ are flown _____ ex - cept _ you a -

lone. _____

1. Goin' to leave ___ this broke - down pal - ace, on my
2., 3. *(See additional lyrics)*

hands and my knees ___ I will roll, _____ roll, roll. ___

Additional Lyrics

2. River gonna take me, sing me sweet and sleepy,
   Sing me sweet and sleepy all the way back home.
   It's a far gone lullaby sung many years ago.
   Mama, Mama, many worlds I've come since I first left home.

Chorus: Goin' home, goin' home.
   By the waterside I will rest my bones.
   Listen to the river sing sweet songs
   To rock my soul.

3. Goin' to plant a weeping willow.
   On the bank's green edge it will grow, grow, grow.
   Sing a lullaby beside the water.
   Lovers come and go; the river roll, roll, roll.

Chorus: Fare you well, fare you well.
   I love you more than words can tell.
   Listen to the river sing sweet songs
   To rock my soul.

BIRD SONG

Words by ROBERT HUNTER
Music by JERRY GARCIA

All I know __ is, some - thing like a bird __ with - in __ her sang. __

All I know, __ she sang __ a lit - tle while __

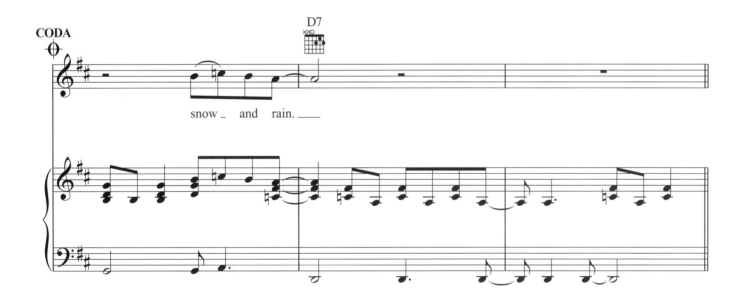

snow __ and rain. ____

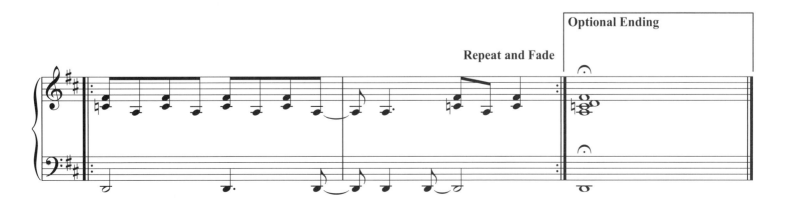

BLACK PETER

Words by ROBERT HUNTER
Music by JERRY GARCIA

All of my __ friends __ come to __ see me last night. __
Fe - ver roll __ up __ to a __ hun - dred and five. __

__ lay - __ ing in my bed and
Roll on __ up, __ gon - na roll back

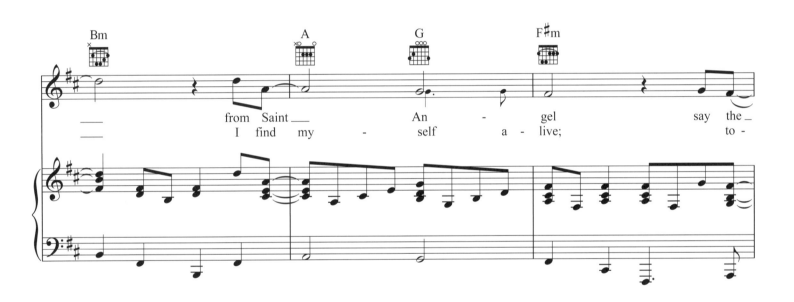

BOX OF RAIN

Words by ROBERT HUNTER
Music by PHIL LESH

BROWN-EYED WOMEN

Words by ROBERT HUNTER
Music by JERRY GARCIA

Moderately bright

Gone ___ are the days when the ox fall down, ___
Nine - teen twen - ty when he ox stepped to the bar. He

take up the yoke ___ and plow ___ the fields a - round.
drank to the dregs ___ of ___ the whis - key jar.

55

CANDYMAN

Words by ROBERT HUNTER
Music by JERRY GARCIA

CASEY JONES

Words by ROBERT HUNTER
Music by JERRY GARCIA

CHINA DOLL

Words by ROBERT HUNTER
Music by JERRY GARCIA

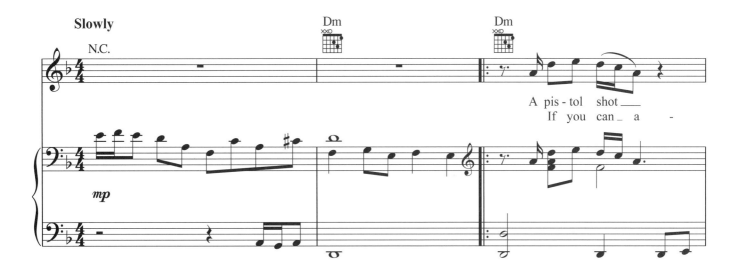

A pis-tol shot ___
If you can a -

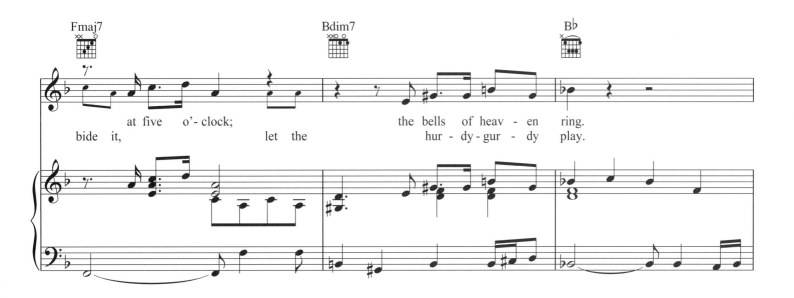

at five o'-clock; let the the bells of heav-en ring.
bide it, let the hur-dy-gur-dy play.

Tell me what you done it for. No, I won't tell you a
Strang-er ones have come by here be - fore they flew a -

CHINA CAT SUNFLOWER

Words by ROBERT HUNTER
Music by JERRY GARCIA

Look for a while at the Chi — na Cat Sun — flow-er,
Cra — zy cat peek-in' through a lace __ ban — dan — na like a
Com — ic book __ col — ors on a vi — o — lin riv — er cry — ing

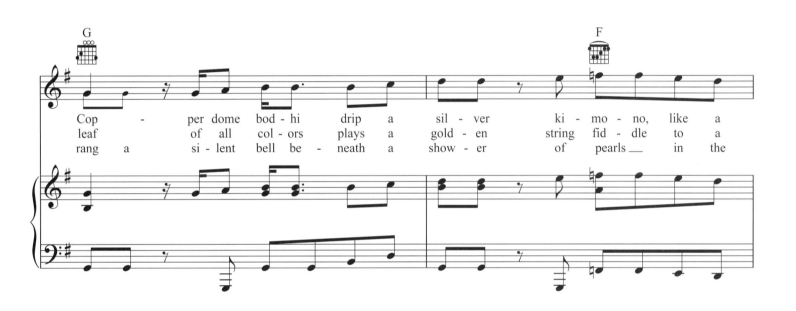

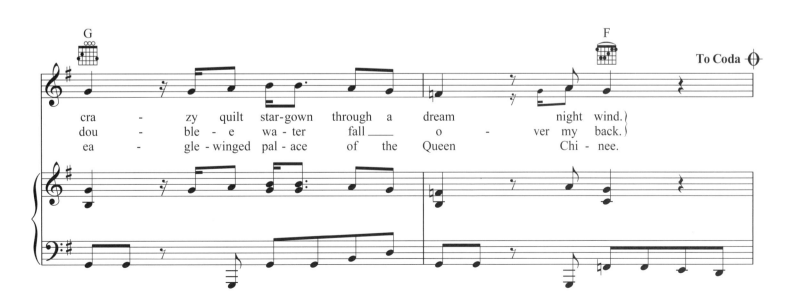

COLD RAIN AND SNOW

Words and Music by JERRY GARCIA,
PHIL LESH, RONALD McKERNAN,
BOB WEIR and WILLIAM KREUTZMANN

Well, she's com-ing down the stairs, __
Well, she went up down to her room __
mar-ried me a wife; __

__ comb-ing back __ her yel-low hair,
and she sang __ a fate-ful tune,
she's been trou-ble all my life.

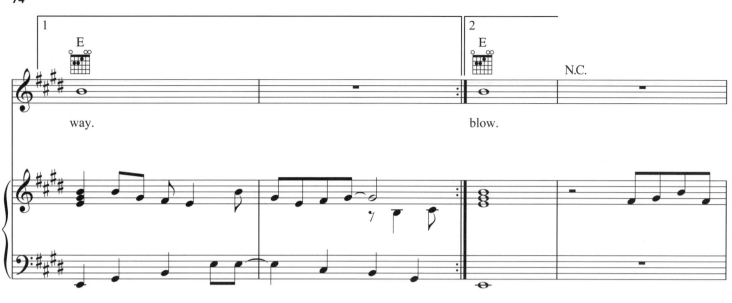

way.   blow.

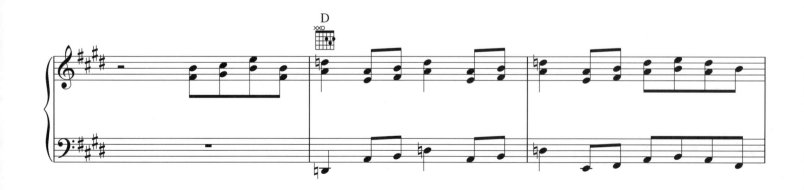

CUMBERLAND BLUES

Words by ROBERT HUNTER
Music by JERRY GARCIA
and PHIL LESH

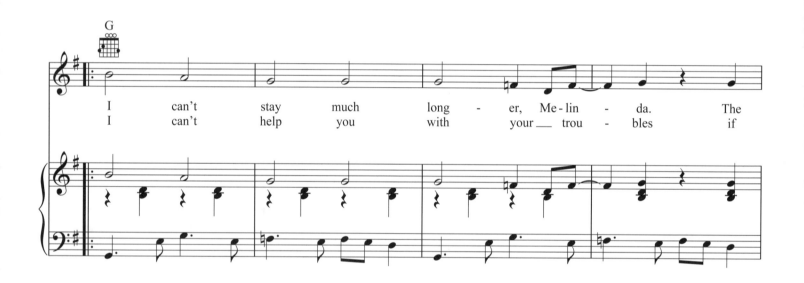

I can't stay much long - er, Me - lin - da. The
I can't help you with your trou - bles if

sun is get - ting high. ____
you won't get help with mine. ____

A lot-ta poor ___ man make a five dol-lar bill; ___

___ will keep him hap-py all ___ the time.

Some oth-er fel-low's mak-ing noth-ing at all, ___

and you can hear_ him cry._

Can I go, bud-dy? Can I go down,_ take your shift at the mine?_

Got-ta get down to the Cum-ber-land mine. (Got-ta get down to the

DARK STAR

Words by ROBERT HUNTER
Music by JERRY GARCIA, MICKEY HART,
BILL KREUTZMANN, PHIL LESH,
RON McKERNAN and BOB WEIR

Dark _____ star crash - es,
Mir - ror shat - ters in

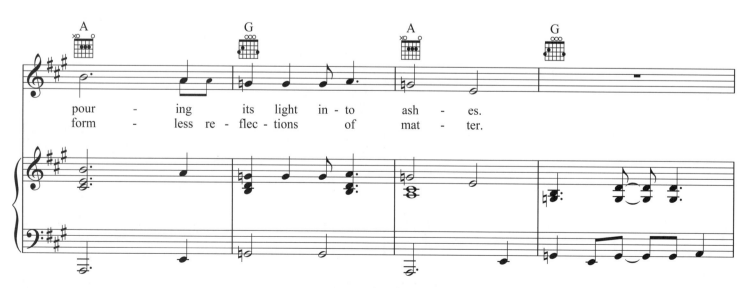

pour - ing its light in - to ash - es.
form - less re - flec - tions of mat - ter.

EASY WIND

Words and Music by
ROBERT HUNTER

Moderate Blues Rock

E7   A7

live five years if I take my time, _____ ball-in' that jack and drink-in' my wine.
Doc-tor say bet-ter stop ball-in' that jack. _ If I live five years, I gon-na bust my back, _____ yes, I

1

E7   A7

I been

2

will.   Eas - y wind _

E7

'cross the bay - ou to - day. _____

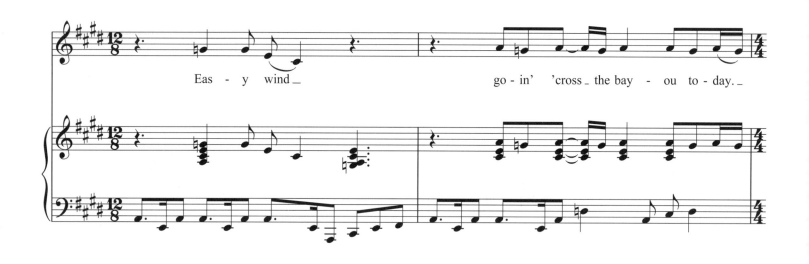

Eas - y wind _ go - in' 'cross _ the bay - ou to - day. _

E7

There's a

A7

whole lot - ta wom-en _ out on the streets in _ red _ to -

day. _____

And the

riv - er keep a - talk - in', __ but you nev - er _____ heard a word __ it said. __

ESTIMATED PROPHET

Words by JOHN BARLOW
Music by BOB WEIR

My time com - in' _____ an - y day; _____ don't wor - ry 'bout ___ me,
My time com - in' _____ an - y day; _____ don't wor - ry 'bout ___ me,
My time com - in' _____ an - y day; _____ don't wor - ry 'bout ___ me,

no.
no.
no.

Been so long I _____ felt this way; _____
It's gon-na be just _____ like they say; _____ them
It's gon-na be just _____ like they say; _____ them

ain't in no hur - ry, no.
voic - es _____ tell _____ me so.
voic - es _____ tell _____ me so.

Rain - bows end down _____
Seems so long I _____
Seems so long I _____

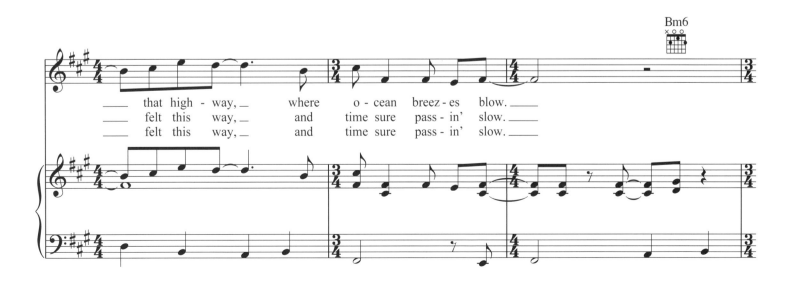

_____ that high - way, _____ where o - cean breez - es blow. _____
_____ felt this way, _____ and time sure pass - in' slow. _____
_____ felt this way, _____ and time sure pass - in' slow. _____

DIRE WOLF

Words by ROBERT HUNTER
Music by JERRY GARCIA

EYES OF THE WORLD

Words by ROBERT HUNTER
Music by JERRY GARCIA

Moderately

Right out-side this __

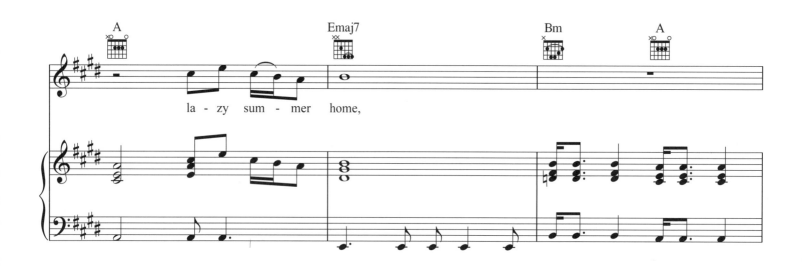

la- zy sum- mer home,

you ain't got time to call your soul a crit- ic, no.

FIRE ON THE MOUNTAIN

Words by ROBERT HUNTER
Music by MICKEY HART

Moderately, in 2

Long - dis - tance run - ner, what you stand - in' there for? __
Al - most a - blaze, __ still you don't feel the heat. __
Long - dis - tance run - ner, what you hold - in' on for? __

Get up, get out, get __
It takes all you got just to
Caught in slow mo - tion in a

* Recorded a half step lower.

out of the door. _____ You're play-in' cold ___
stay on the beat. _____ You say ___ it's a
dash to the door. _____ The flame ___ from your

mu - sic on the bar - room floor, ___
liv - in'; we all got - ta eat. ___
stage has now spread to the floor. ___

drowned in your laugh - ter and dead to the core. ___
But you're here a - lone; there's no one to com - pete. ___
You gave all you had; why you want to give more? ___

FRANKLIN'S TOWER

Words by ROBERT HUNTER
Music by JERRY GARCIA and BILL KREUTZMANN

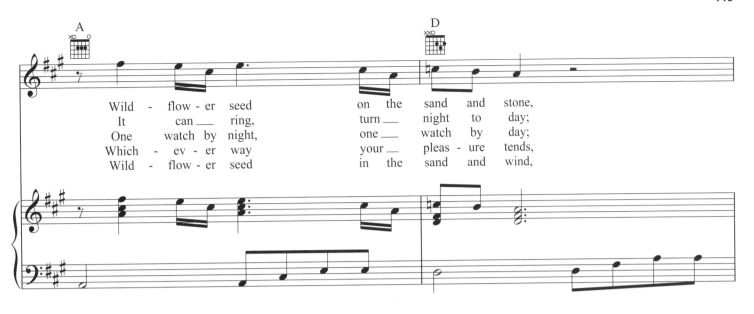

Wild - flow - er seed on the sand and stone,
It can ___ ring, turn ___ night to day;
One watch by night, one ___ watch by day;
Which - ev - er way your ___ pleas - ure tends,
Wild - flow - er seed in the sand and wind,

may the four ___ winds blow ___ you safe - ly home.
it can ring like fire ___ when ___ you lose your way.
if you get con - fused, ___ lis - ten to the mu - sic play.
if you plant ice, ___ you're gon - na har - vest wind.
may the four ___ winds blow ___ you home a - gain.

Roll a - way the dew. ___ Roll a - way the

THE GOLDEN ROAD

Words and Music by JERRY GARCIA,
BILL KREUTZMANN, PHIL LESH,
RON McKERNAN and BOB WEIR

Moderately fast

See that girl___ bare-foot-in' a-long?___
Ev-'ry-bod-y's danc-in' in a ring a-round the sun.
Take a va-ca-tion, fall out for a while.___

Whis-t'lin' and   sing-in', she's a car-ry-in' on._____   Got
No-bod-y's   fin-ished; we ain't e-ven be-gun._____   So
Sum-mer's com-in' in_____   and it's go-in' out-ta style.   Well,

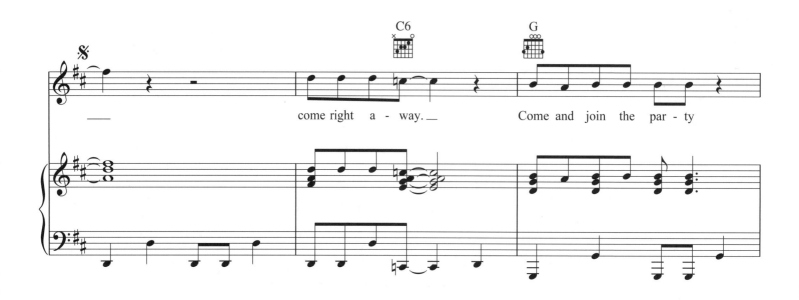

FRIEND OF THE DEVIL

Words by ROBERT HUNTER
Music by JERRY GARCIA and JOHN DAWSON

Moderately bright, in 2

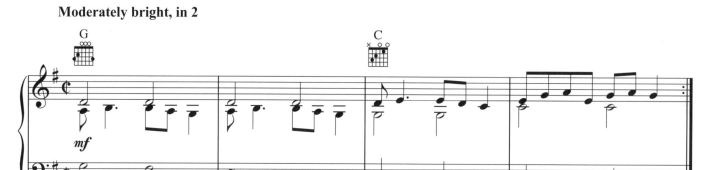

I lit out ___ from Re - no; I ___ was trailed ___ by twen - ty hounds. ___
Ran in - to ___ the dev - il, babe; ___ he loaned ___ me twen - ty bills. ___

___ Did - n't get ___ to sleep ___ that night till the
___ Spent the night ___ in U - tah in a cave

friend of mine. ___ If I get home ___ be - fore ___ day - light, I

just might get some sleep ___ to - night. ___

Got two rea - sons why I cry ___ a - way ___ each lone - ly night. ___

HELL IN A BUCKET

Words by JOHN BARLOW
Music by BRENT MYDLAND and BOB WEIR

Well, I was drink-ing last night___ with a bik-er,___
Sweet Lit- tle Soft - core Pre - tend - er,___
You must real - ly con - sid - er the cir - cus,___

* *Recorded a half step lower.*

HIGH TIME

Words by ROBERT HUNTER
Music by JERRY GARCIA

Moderately slow

1. You told me good - bye. _____
2.–4. *(See additional lyrics)*

How_ was I _____ to know _____

you did - n't mean_ good - bye? _____

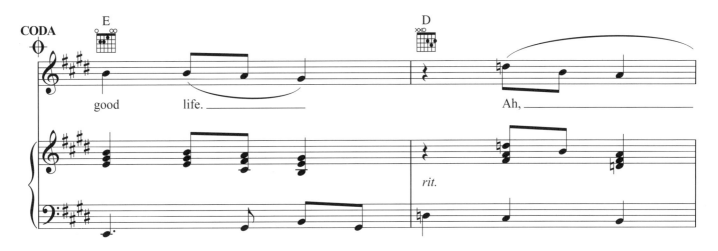

good life. _____ Ah, _____

well, _____ I _____ know.

Additional Lyrics

2. The wheels are muddy,
   Got a ton of hay.
   Now, listen here, baby,
   'Cause I mean what I say.
   I'm having a hard time
   Living the good life.
   Ah, well, I know.

3. Tomorrow come trouble,
   Tomorrow come pain.
   Now, don't think too hard, baby,
   'Cause you know what I'm saying.
   I could show you a high time,
   Living the good life.
   Ah, don't be that way.

4. Nothing's for certain;
   It could always go wrong.
   Come in when it's raining,
   Go on out when it's gone.
   We could have us a high time,
   Living the good life.
   Ah, well, I know.

I KNOW YOU RIDER

Traditional
Arranged by JERRY GARCIA, KEITH GODCHAUX,
WILLIAM KREUTZMANN, PHIL LESH,
RONALD McKERNAN and BOB WEIR

Moderately, in 2

I

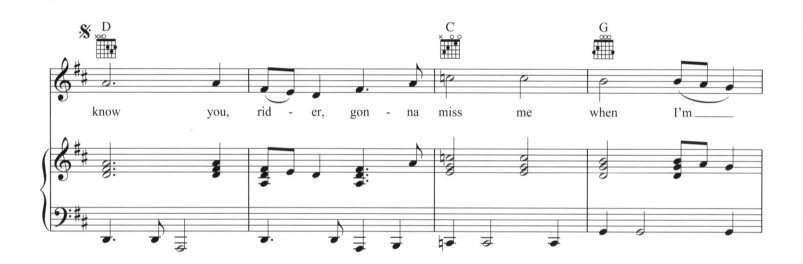

know you, rid - er, gon - na miss me when I'm

gone. I

144

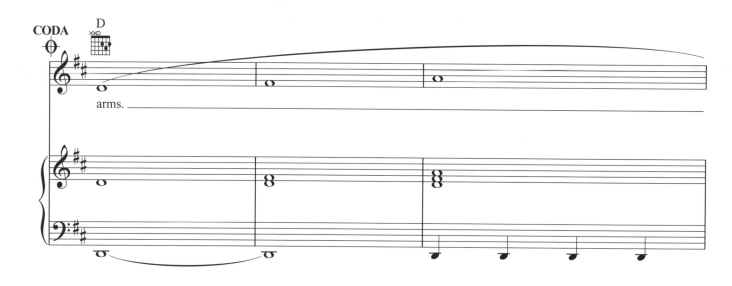

arms.

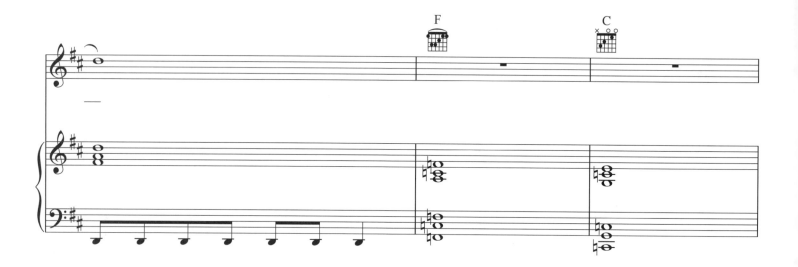

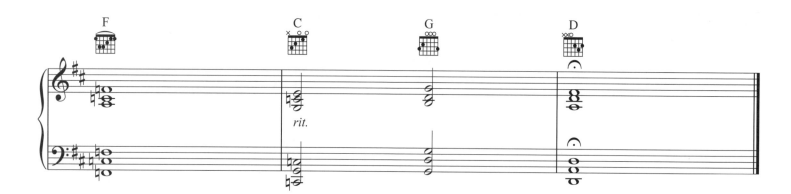

rit.

Additional Lyrics

2. The sun will shine in my back door someday.
   The sun will shine in my back door someday.
   March winds will blow all my troubles away.

3. I wish I was a headlight on a northbound train.
   I wish I was a headlight on a northbound train.
   I'd shine my light through the cool Colorado rain.

JACK STRAW

Words by ROBERT HUNTER
Music by BOB WEIR

Moderately slow, in 2

We can share the wom-en, we can share the wine. _____
Leav-in' Tex - as, fourth day _____ of _____ Ju - ly. _____

We can share what we got of yours, _____ 'cause we
Sun so hot, the clouds _____ so low, _____ the

done shared all _____ of _____ mine. _____
ea - gles filled _____ the _____ sky. _____

We used to play   for sil -
Jack __ Straw   from Wich -

- ver; now __ we play for   life.
- i - ta cut his bud - dy   down

LOOKS LIKE RAIN

Words by JOHN BARLOW
Music by BOB WEIR

1. I woke to - day, _____
2., 3. (See additional lyrics)

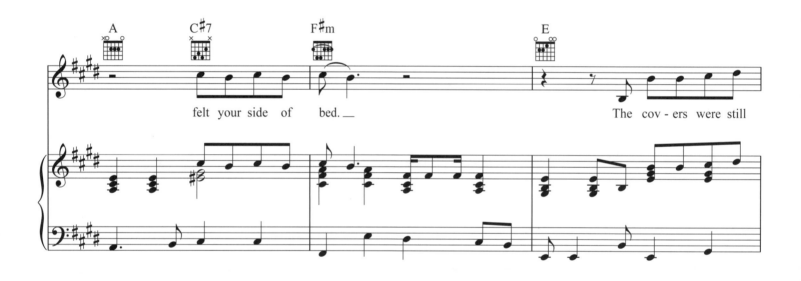

felt your side of bed. ___ The cov - ers were still

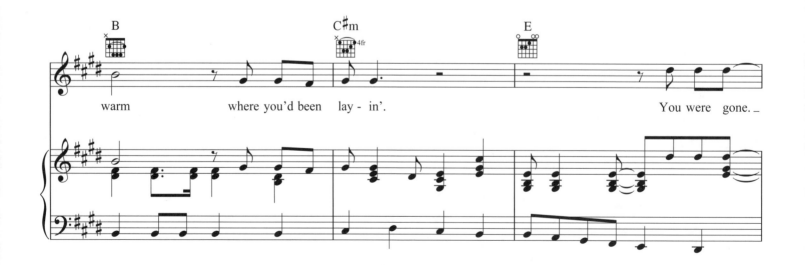

warm   where you'd been lay - in'.   You were gone. ___

Yes, and brave the storm to come, ___ for it
sure - ly looks like rain.

I can't stand the rain.

rit.

Additional Lyrics

2. Did you ever waken to the sound of street cats making love?
   You'd guess from the cries you were listening to a fight.
   Well, you know, oh no, hate's the last thing they're thinking of.
   You know they're only tryin' to make it through the night.

3. I only want to hold you; I don't want to tie you down
   Or fence you in the lines I might've drawn.
   It's just that I, oh, I have gotten used to havin' you around.
   The landscape would be empty if you were gone.

ME & MY UNCLE

Words and Music by
JOHN PHILLIPS

Em

West Tex - as bound. ___ We ___ stopped o -
or - dered drinks for all. ___ Three days ___ in the sad -
they're load - ed down. ___ So soon ___ af - ter pay -

G **Em**

- ver in San - ta Fe, ___
- dle, you know, my bod - y hurt. ___
- day; you know, it seemed a shame. ___

G

that be - in' the point ___ just a - bout half -
It be - in' ___ sum - mer, I took off my
You know, ___ my un - cle, he starts a friend - ly

A7 **Em**

way. Hey, ___ and you know, it was the
shirt and I ___ tried to wash off ___
game; yeah, ___ High - Low Jack, and the

MISSISSIPPI HALF-STEP UPTOWN TOODELOO

Words by ROBERT HUNTER
Music by JERRY GARCIA

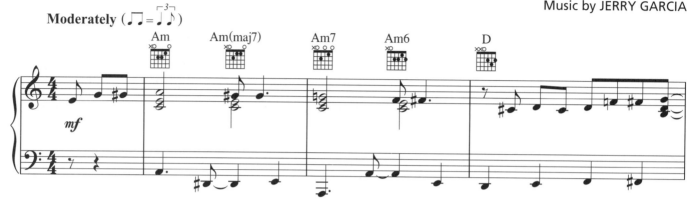

On the day when I _____ was born, _____
If all you got to live _____ for ____
They say that when your ship ____ comes in, ____

Dad-dy sat down and cried. _____
is what you left be-hind, _____
first ____ man takes the sails, _____

I had the mark just as
get your-self a
sec-ond takes the

(Walk Me Out in the)
MORNING DEW

Words and Music by BONNIE DOBSON
and TIM ROSE

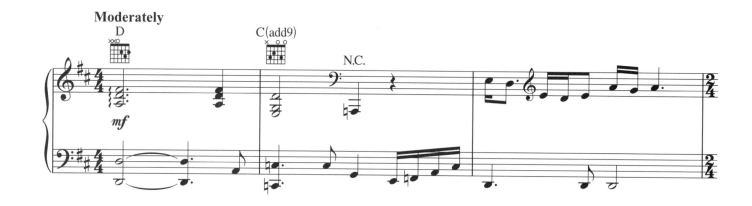

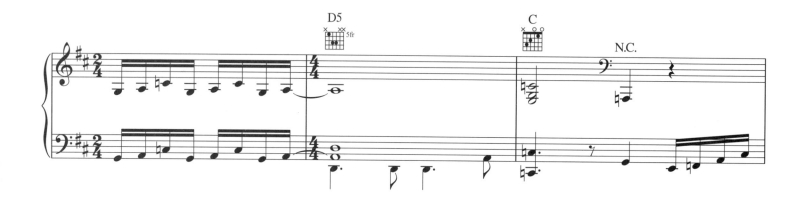

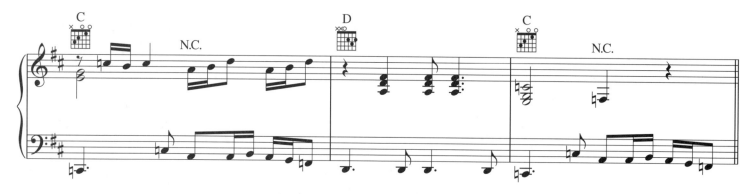

169

172

THE MUSIC NEVER STOPPED

Words by JOHN BARLOW
Music by BOB WEIR

Moderately bright

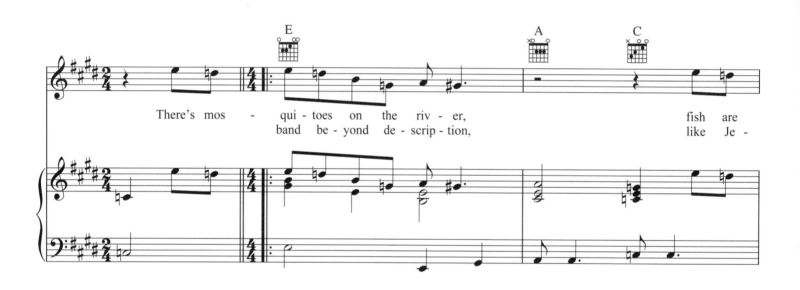

There's mos - qui - toes on the riv - er,   fish are
band be - yond de - scrip - tion,   like Je -

ris - ing up like birds. _____   It's been
ho - vah's fa - v'rite choir. _____   Peo - ple

It's a rain - bow ___ full of sound,
No one's no - ticed, but the band's all packed and gone.

it's

fire - works, cal - li - o - pes and clowns. ___
Was it ev - er here at all? ___

Ev - 'ry - bod - y's
But they kept on

danc - in'.
danc - in'.

Come on, chil - dren.
Come on, chil - dren.

Come on, chil - dren.
Come on, chil - dren.

NEW SPEEDWAY BOOGIE

Words by ROBERT HUNTER
Music by JERRY GARCIA

Moderate Shuffle

Please ___ don't dom - i - nate the rap, Jack, if you got ___

___ noth - ing new ___ to say. ___ If ___ you please, ___ don't back

up the track;— this train's— got— to run— to-day.— I

spent a lit-tle time on the moun-tain,_____ spent a lit-tle time— on the hill.—

— I heard some say, "Bet-ter run a-way." Oth-

can de - ny,__ who can de - ny__ it's not__ just a change in style?__

One step done and an - oth - er be - gun,__ and I won-

- der how__ man - y miles.__ I spent a lit - tle time on the

moun - tain,_____ spent a lit - tle time_ on the hill.__ Things_

may-be find out be - fore ___ too long. _____

One way or an - oth - er,

one way or an - oth - er, one way or an -

oth - er, this dark - ness got to give. ___

Repeat and Fade

Optional Ending

OPERATOR

Words and Music by
RON McKERNAN

Moderately fast

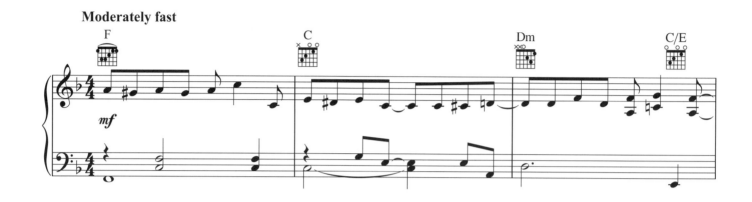

Op - er - a - tor,
think she's__ some - where

can you help me?__ Help me, if you please.__
down south, down a - bout Bat - on Rouge.__ But

It's flood-ing down in Tex-as, the poles __
I don't __ know where she's go-ing, I don't care __

__ are down in U-tah. Got to find a pri-vate line. __
__ where she's been, long as she's been do-ing it right, __

She

long as she's been do-ing it right. __

PLAYING IN THE BAND

Words by ROBERT HUNTER
Music by MICHAEL HART and BOB WEIR

Some folks trust to rea - son, oth - ers trust to might.
Some folks look for an - swers, oth - ers look for fights.
Stand - in' on a tow - er, world at my com - mand.

I don't trust to noth - in', but I know it come out right.
Some folks up in tree - tops just to look to see the sights.
You just keep a-turn - in' while I'm play - ing in the band.

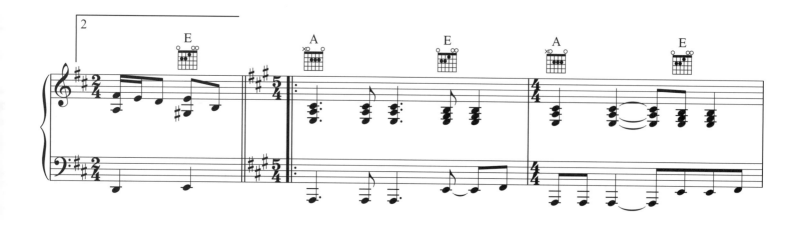

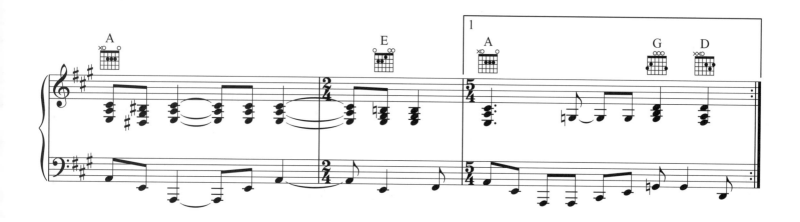

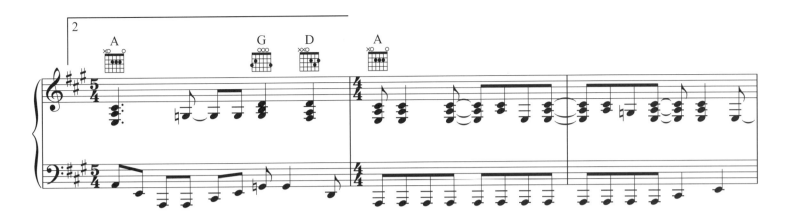

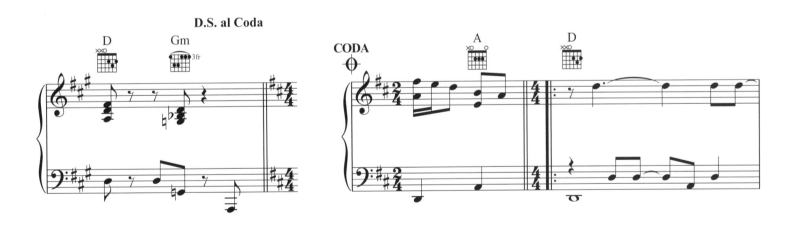

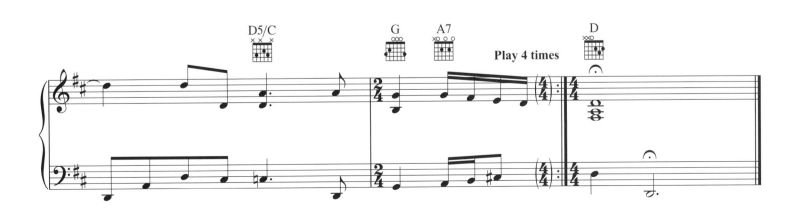

RAMBLE ON ROSE

Words by ROBERT HUNTER
Music by JERRY GARCIA

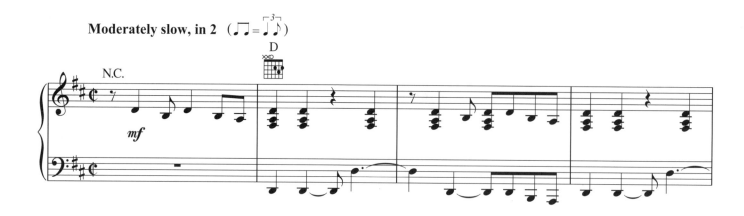

Just like Jack the Rip - per,
Just like Jack and Jill, _____
Just like Cra - zy Ot - to,

just like Mo - jo Hand, _____ just like _____ Bil - ly Sun
Ma - ma told the sail - or, "One heat up and one cool
just like Wolf - man Jack, _____ sit - tin' plush with a roy -

-day   in a shot - gun rag - time band._____
____ down.   Leave noth - in' for the tai - lor."__
al flush,   ac - es back to back._____

Just like   New York Cit - y,
Just like   Jack and Jill, ___
Just like   Mar - y Shel - ley,

just like   Jer - i - cho, ____   pace the halls __ and
Pa - pa   told the jail - er,   "One go up __ and
just like   Frank - en - stein, ___   clank your chains_ and

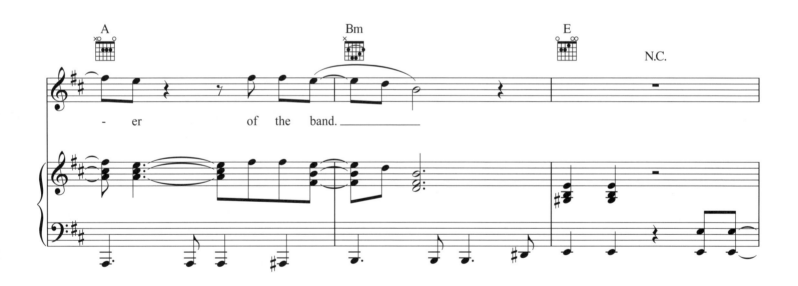

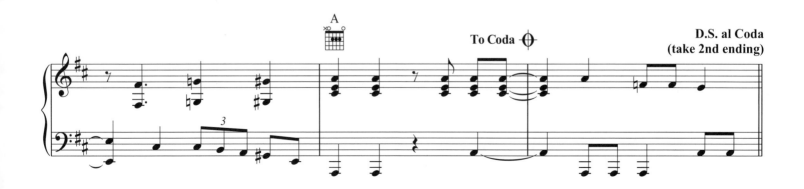

A
1
D
Ram-ble on, Rose.
2, 3
D
A♯+
Bm
Rose.
I'm gon-na sing
C
you
a hun-dred vers-es in rag-time.
Bm
C
I know this song;
it ain't
nev-er gon-na
3

ONE MORE SATURDAY NIGHT

Words and Music by
BOB WEIR

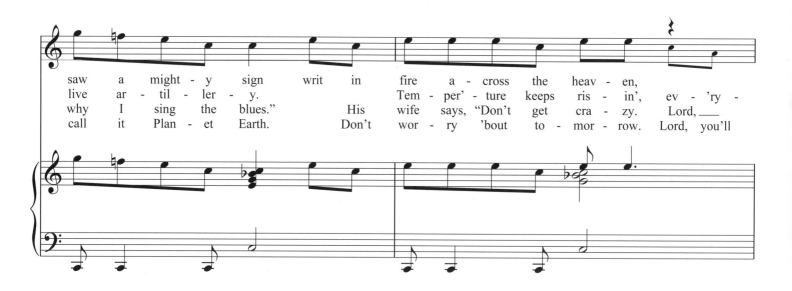

saw a might - y sign writ in fire a - cross the heav - en,
live ar - til - ler - y. Tem - per' - ture keeps ris - in', ev - 'ry -
why I sing the blues." His wife says, "Don't get cra - zy. Lord, ___
call it Plan - et Earth. Don't wor - ry 'bout to - mor - row. Lord, you'll

plain as black and white: "Get pre - pared. There's gon - na be a
bod - y get - tin' high. Come the rock - in' stroke of mid - night, the whole
you know what to do. ___ Just crank that old Vic - tro - la, ___ put
know ___ when it comes: when the rock - in', roll - in' mu - sic meets the

par - ty to - night." ___
place is gon - na fly.   Uh - huh. ___
on your rock - in' shoes."
ris - in', shin - in' sun.

RIPPLE

Words by ROBERT HUNTER
Music by JERRY GARCIA

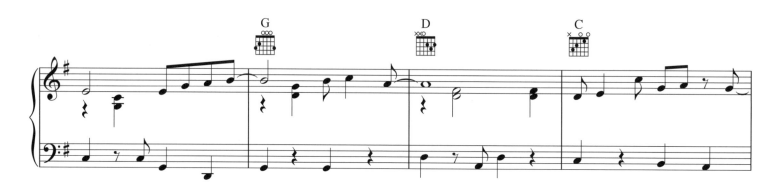

ROSEMARY

Words by ROBERT HUNTER
Music by JERRY GARCIA

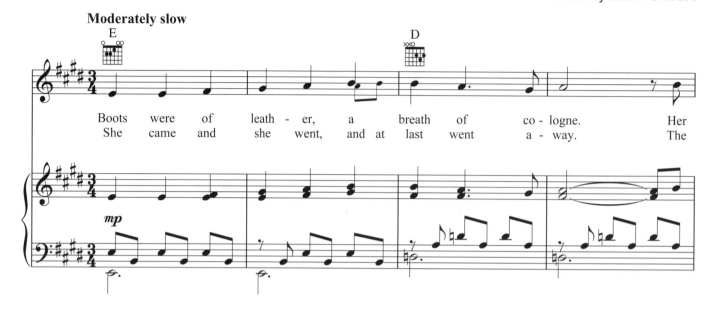

Boots were of leath-er, a breath of co-logne. Her
She came and she went, and at last went a-way. The

mir-ror was a win-dow she sat by a-lone.
gar-den was sealed _ when the flow-ers de-cayed.

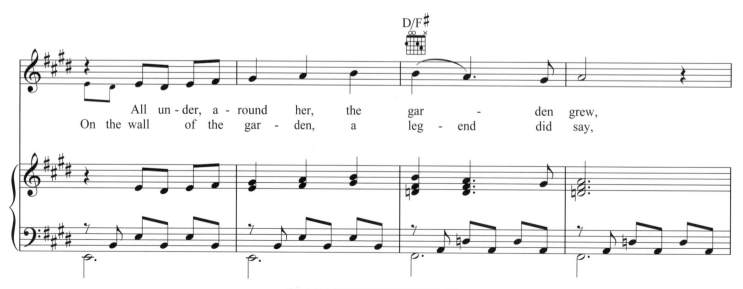

All un-der, a-round her, the gar - den grew,
On the wall of the gar-den, a leg-end did say,

ST. STEPHEN

Words by JERRY GARCIA and PHIL LESH
Music by ROBERT HUNTER

219

you have spurned.   Sev -'ral sea - sons   with their trea - sons

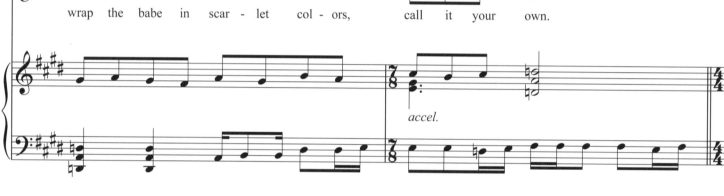

wrap the babe in scar - let col - ors,   call it your own.

accel.

A little faster

Did he doubt or did he try? An - swers a - plen - ty in the by and by.
Saint __ Ste - phen will re - main. All he's __ lost __ he __ shall re - gain.

Talk a - bout your plen - ty, talk __ a - bout your ills. One man gath-ers what an - oth - er man spills.
Sea - shore __ washed by the suds __ and the foam, been

SCARLET BEGONIAS

Words by ROBERT HUNTER
Music by JERRY GARCIA

Moderately, in 2

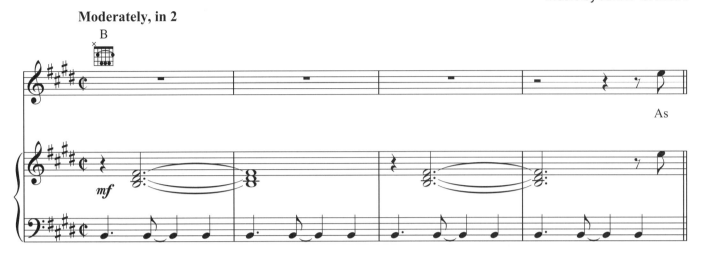

As

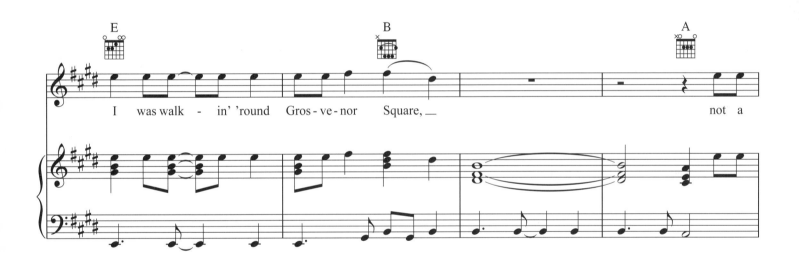

I was walk - in' 'round Gros - ve - nor Square, ___ not a

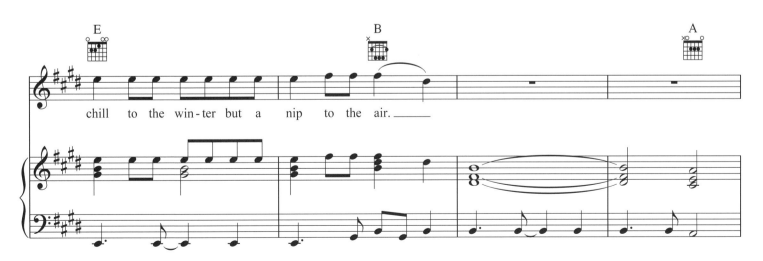

chill to the win - ter but a nip to the air. ___

Once in a while,__ you get shown__ the light in the strang-est of plac - es if you

look at it right.

Well, there

I had to learn the hard way to let ___ her pass
Ev - 'ry - bod - y is play - ing in the heart of gold

by, let her pass by.
band, heart of gold

The band.

Repeat and Fade

Optional Ending

SHAKEDOWN STREET

Words by ROBERT HUNTER
Music by JERRY GARCIA

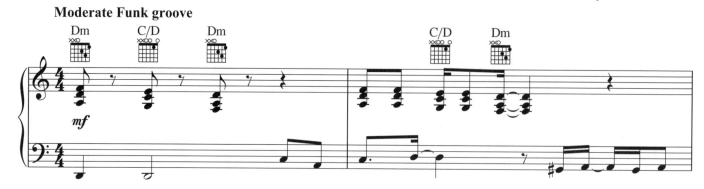

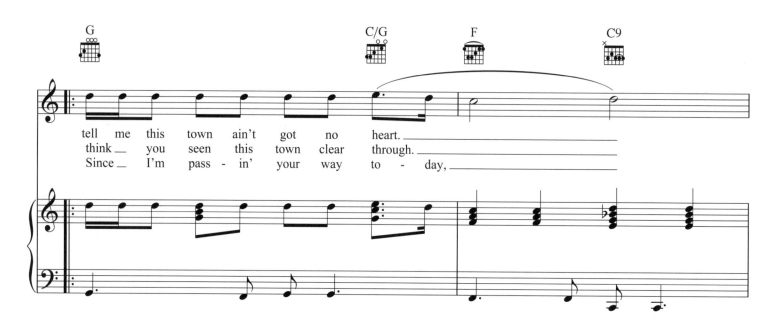

tell me this town ain't got no heart.
think __ you seen this town clear through.
Since __ I'm pass - in' your way to - day,

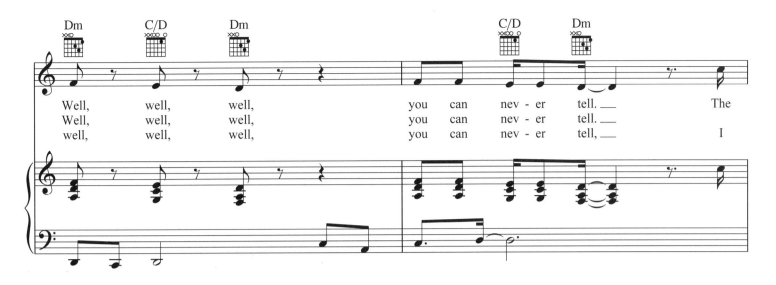

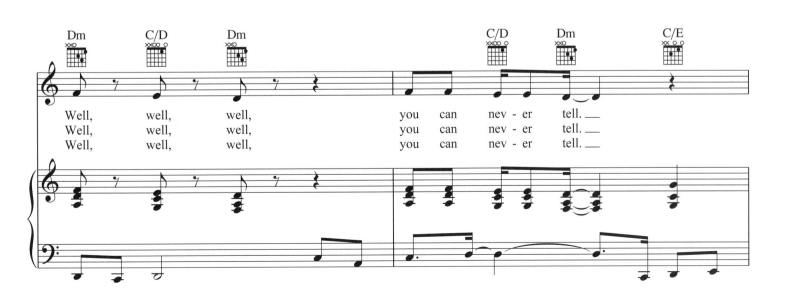

SHIP OF FOOLS

Words by ROBERT HUNTER
Music by JERRY GARCIA

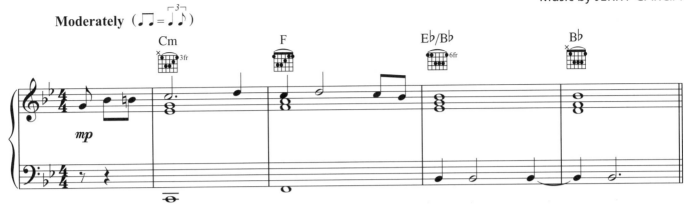

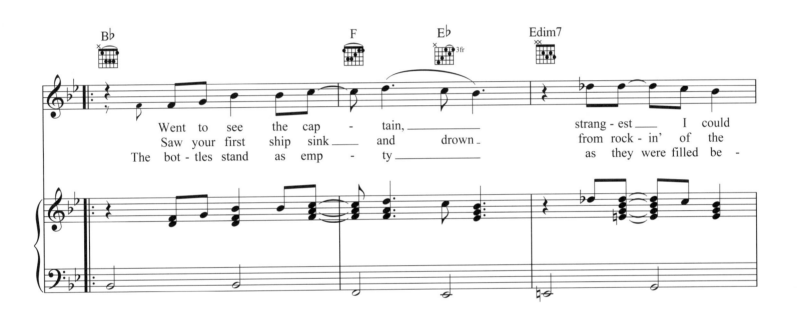

STELLA BLUE

Words by ROBERT HUNTER
Music by JERRY GARCIA

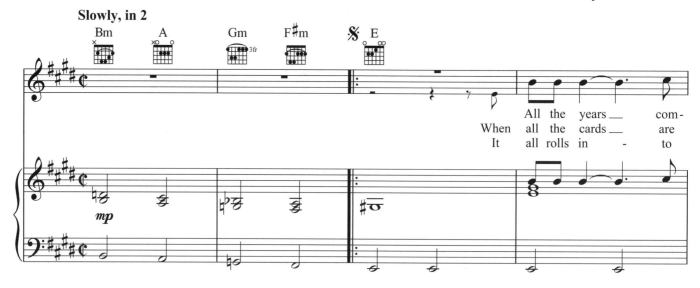

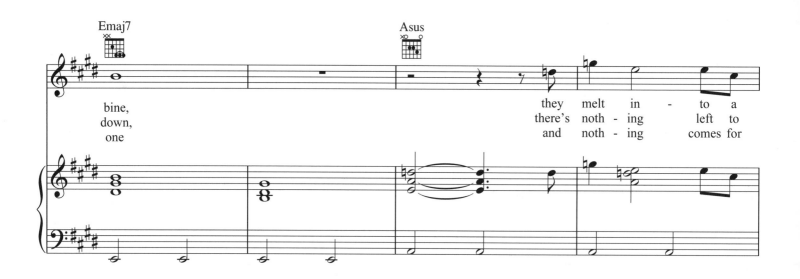

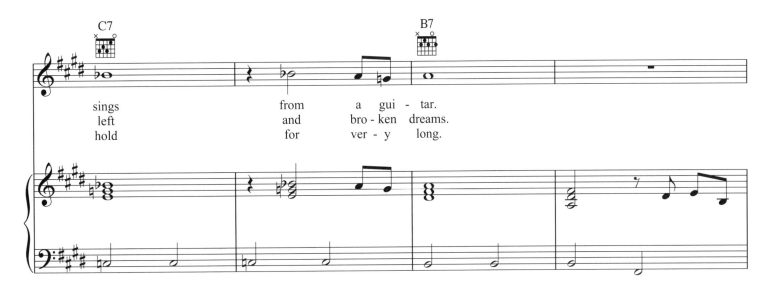

sings
left
hold

from
and
for

a
bro - ken
ver - y

gui - tar.
dreams.
long.

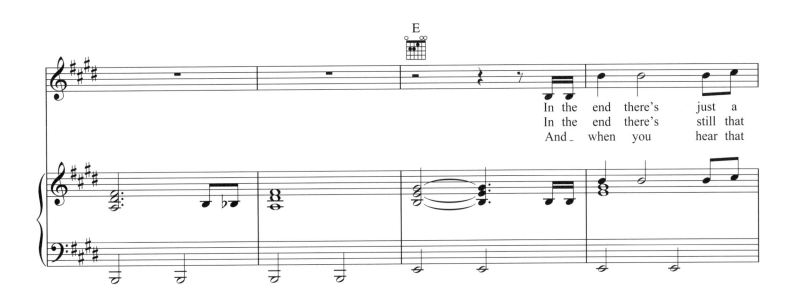

In the end there's   just a
In the end there's   still that
And _ when you   hear that

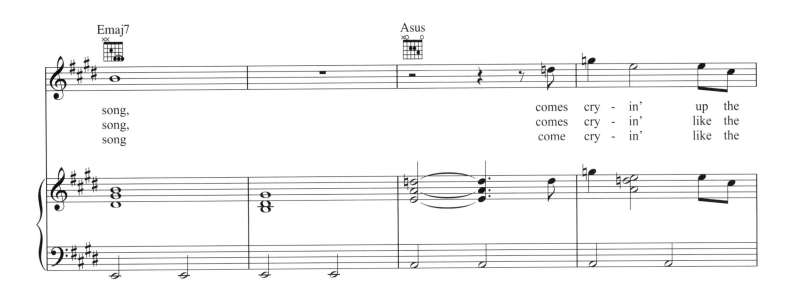

song,
song,
song

comes cry - in'   up the
comes cry - in'   like the
come cry - in'   like the

Gon - na make them shine. _____

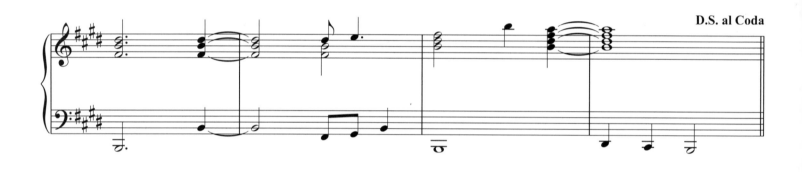

D.S. al Coda

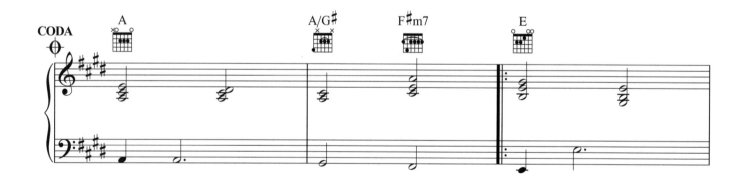

Repeat and Fade | **Optional Ending**

SUGAREE

Words by ROBERT HUNTER
Music by JERRY GARCIA

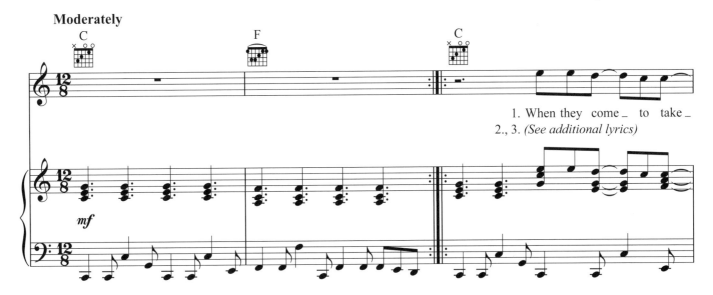

1. When they come _ to take _
2., 3. *(See additional lyrics)*

_ you _ down, _   when they bring _ that wag - on 'round,

when they come _ to call ___ on you ___

Additional Lyrics

2. You thought you was the cool fool
   And never could do no wrong.
   You had everything sewed up tight.
   How come you lay awake all night long?

3. Well, in spite of all you gained,
   You still have to stand out in the pouring rain.
   One last voice is calling you,
   And I guess it's time you go.

SUGAR MAGNOLIA

Words by ROBERT HUNTER
Music by BOB WEIR

Moderately fast

Sug-ar Mag-no - lia, blos-soms bloom-ing, heads all emp-ty and I____ ____don't care.____ Saw my ba-by down____ by the riv-er;

TERRAPIN STATION

Words by ROBERT HUNTER
Music by JERRY GARCIA

TILL THE MORNING COMES

Words by ROBERT HUNTER
Music by JERRY GARCIA

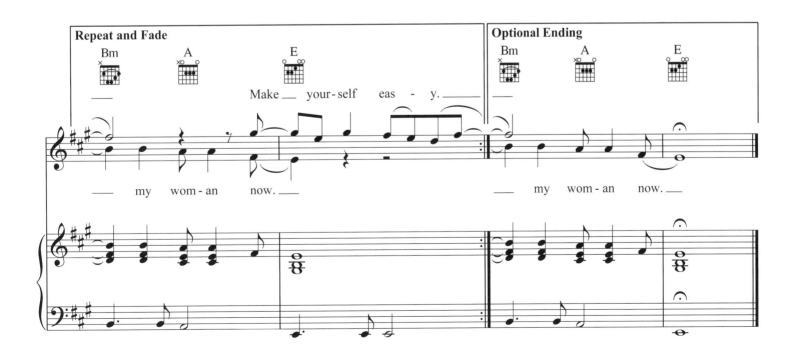

TOUCH OF GREY

Words by ROBERT HUNTER
Music by JERRY GARCIA

Recorded a half step higher.

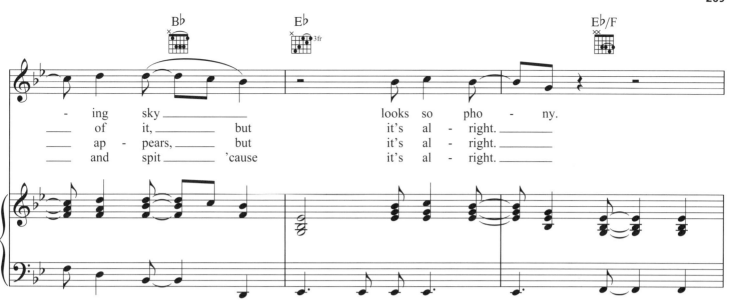

-ing sky _____ looks so pho - ny.
____ of it, _____ but it's al - right. _____
____ ap - pears, _____ but it's al - right. _____
____ and spit _____ 'cause it's al - right. _____

Dawn is break - ing ev - 'ry - where. Light a can - dle, curse _
Sor - ry that __ you feel ____ that __ way. __ The on - ly thing_ there is ___
Cows giv - ing ker - o - sene, __ kid can't read __ at sev -
Oh, well, a touch __ of __ grey, __ kind - a suits__ you an -

____ the __ glare. _ Draw the cur - tains, I _____ don't care _____ 'cause
____ to __ say: __ Ev - 'ry sil - ver lin - ing's got _____ a
- en - teen. _ The words he knows are all ____ ob - scene, _____ but
- y __ way. __ That was all I had ____ to say, _____ and

by. _____ I will ___ sur - vive. _____

I will ___ sur - vive. _____

WHARF RAT

Words by ROBERT HUNTER
Music by JERRY GARCIA

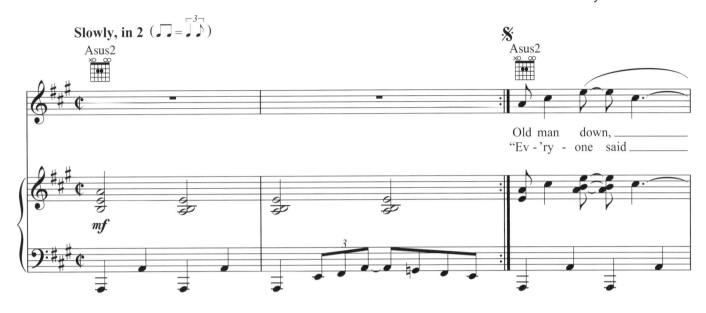

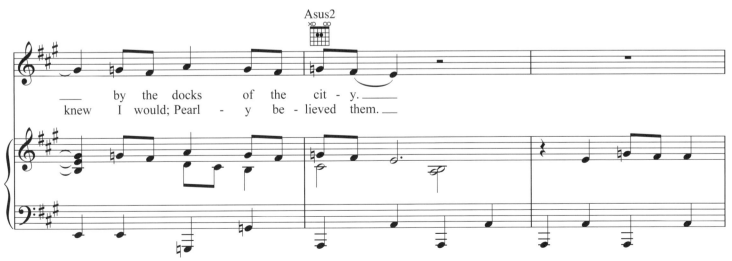

276

sure she's _____ been." _____
know that girl's been _____ true to me.

I

Em

D

Asus2

I said to him, "I'm sure she's _____ been true to you."
know she's _____ been, I'm sure she's _____ been true to me.

1

I

2

Repeat and Fade

Optional Ending

TRUCKIN'

Words by ROBERT HUNTER
Music by JERRY GARCIA,
PHIL LESH and BOB WEIR

UNCLE JOHN'S BAND

Words by ROBERT HUNTER
Music by JERRY GARCIA

VICTIM OR THE CRIME

Words by GERRIT GRAHAM
Music by BOB WEIR

Pa-tience runs out on the junk-ie,
Like him, I'm tired of tryin' to heal

the dark side hires an-oth-er soul. ___
this tom-cat heart with which I'm blessed. ___

Did he steal his fate or
Is de-struc-tion lov-ing's